Shops

To market, to market,
To buy a plum bun.
Home again, home again,
Market is done.

Activity 1

Old and new ways of buying and selling

Do you like shopping?

Do you have a favourite shop?

If your favourite shop was not there how could you buy what you needed?

Find out and make a collection of ways you have thought of. These are inventions.

Long ago, before shops were invented, people exchanged things in order to get what they needed.

Markets were very important for buying and selling in the past.

Have you a market in your town?

Are markets a good place to shop?

Set up a market stall in your classroom.

★ What will you sell?

★ How will you sell?

Invent a market voice.

Which shop do people like?

People shop at different shops.

At the village shop.

At the supermarket.

At the hypermarket.

At the town market.

Have you these in your town?

★ How are they the same?
★ How are they different?

Make a simple map of where you live.
Show where the nearest shops are.

Find out where people shop most for food.
Make a survey.

★ Why do they use that shop?
★ What do they like?
★ What don't they like?

Activity 3

At the supermarket

Work in teams of 2 or 3.
Find out about the different goods which are sold in food shops.
How many different kinds of goods are there?

Think up different ways of sorting the goods.

You will need

empty supermarket packages

These packages can be your pretend goods.

Can you think of other ways of sorting?

Discuss which goods you like best.
Which is the most popular product?

Supermarkets have systems

The supermarket has systems to help people to buy the goods.

There is the trolley system.

Find out what happens to a trolley.

Design and make a flow chart and talk about what happens to a trolley.

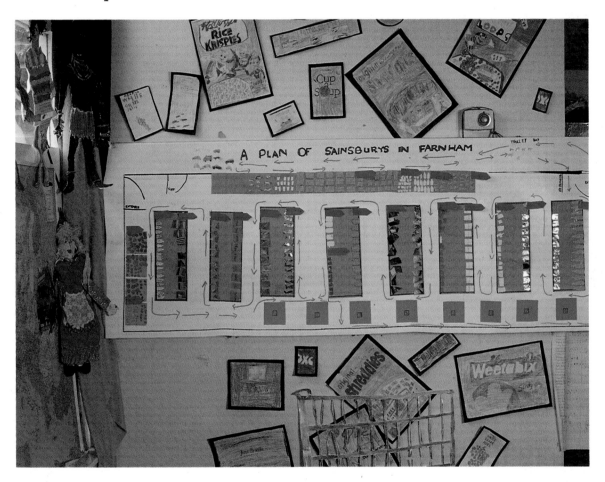

Is it a good system? Do we need it?

Can you improve it or invent something better?

What are the problems?

Think up some ideas of new systems.

Try a few out.

Which idea was best?

Activity 5

Buying and selling

Problem

Invent a food shop with a shop sign which people will like.
Work in a team of two or three. You have 30 minutes.

You will need

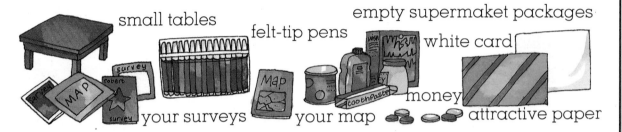

small tables felt-tip pens empty supermaket packages

your surveys your map white card money attractive paper

Work in a team of two or three. You have 30 minutes.

★ What kind of a shop might be best?
★ Where will your shop be?
★ What will you sell?
★ What about prices?
★ Will it make you want to buy?

Talk over some ideas first.
Are you ready?
Make it.

Let the other groups come and buy at your shop.
Have you all got a job to do in your shop?
Did you make a good shop?
What do your customers think?

Why do things look like they do?

Collect

packaged food inventions

Look at a can of beans and
ask yourself questions about it.

★ Why does it look like it does?
★ What is it made out of?

Use a magnet to find out what
metal the can is made from.
Why isn't it made out of gold,
plastic or card?
Where does the metal come
from?

Could beans be packaged in a different way?
Could you put baked beans in a packet?
Try it out!

Look at another food invention.
Think up questions and tests!

Bottles and tins

Packaging is an invention which helps to keep food fresh. This is a picture of a very old advertisment for a tin of baked beans. It is 90 years old.

Canning is still used as a way of keeping food fresh.
Bottling is another way of keeping food fresh.
Both these ways of keeping food have been used for a long time.

Look at fruit in a tin and in a jar.

★ What are the good and bad points of the tin?
★ What are the good and bad points of the jar?

Can you think which packaging is a newer invention than canning or bottling?

Milk

This is a caveman.
He lived 4000 years ago.
How do you think he stored his milk?

He might have used a goatskin.
Can you find something which you might use for a goatskin?

Collect

things which can help you keep milk and things made from milk.

★Think about the good points.
★Think about the bad points.

Some ways to help you keep milk will be modern.
Some ways will be old fashioned.

Ask your milkman which way he likes best!

Activity 9

Visit a dairy

What does the dairy section of the supermarket sell?
Have you wondered how the food gets from the cow to the supermarket?

Perhaps you can visit your local dairy.
Look at people's jobs.
Ask the people about their jobs.

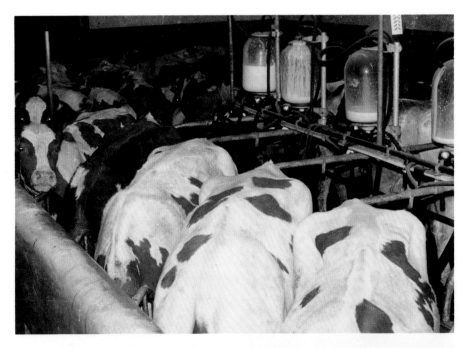

Back in school, design and make a large flow chart of how the food travels from the cow to the supermarket. Start with the cow and finish with the shop.

Tell another class about how this system works. Why is it important to make sure everything is done quickly?

What's in a bag?

You will need

two packet of crisps

plate

Why do crisps need a packet?

Open one of the packets of crisps. Leave a few crisps overnight out of a packet to find out if they really do need a packet.

The next day taste a crisp from the unopened packet and taste one which was left out of the opened packet.

Make it a fair test. How do you do this?

You have to try and change only one thing.

Make a chart to show how you will keep everything fair.

Did they taste different?

Did one crisp go soggy?

Soggy things soak up water. Where does the water come from to make crisps soggy?

Activity 11

Inventions to stop drying up!

If things are left unwrapped, some go soggy while others dry up.
How can you test this?
Remember to keep everything fair.

Make a chart showing which things dry up and which things go soggy.

Things which go dry.	Things which go soggy.
bread Cake Cheese Sandwiches buns	Crisps biscuits monster Manch hula hoops crisp - bread

Talk with your class about why some things lose water and why some things gain water. Isn't that strange?

Choose one thing which goes soggy and one which dries up. Invent something to keep the water in or out!

You will need
your choice of materials from the junk box

Test your invention on your food.
Does it work?

Inventors need to know about materials.

Beautiful packaging

Inventors are interested in
keeping food fresh.
Inventors are also interested
in making food look attractive.

Do you like pretty and unusual
packaging?
What is its purpose?

Collect
pretty and unusual
packaging

Make a display of all the
packages you have
collected.
Does the package make
you want to buy the goods?

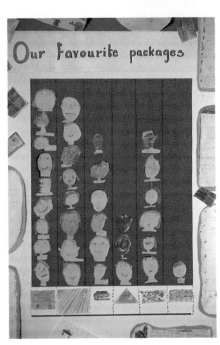

Look at each one in turn.
Look at the colour
            the shape
            the size.

Which is your favourite
package?
Do you all like the same
package or do you all have
different favourites?

Activity 13

I am an inventor!

Problem

Invent your own beautiful and unusual package for something.

You will need

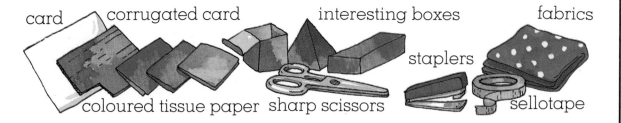

card   corrugated card   interesting boxes   fabrics

coloured tissue paper   sharp scissors   staplers   sellotape

Work with a friend.

Choose what you want to package.

Think about the problem.

What might people like?

Look at the materials.

Ideas! Ideas! Ideas!

Draw some of your best ideas.

Making and testing

Think about the materials you are going to use.
How are you going to cut or join them?
Ask your teacher if you need help.

Make your idea.
Have you any problems?
How can you solve them?

Tell everyone how you made your idea.

★ Which materials did you use?
★ Why did you choose those?
★ How did you cut and join them?

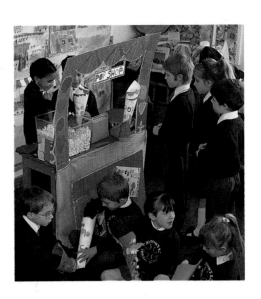

Put all your packages into your shop.
Ask another class to be customers to your shop.

Activity 15

Taking stock

Have you a lot of stock now in your shop?
Do you know what stock you have?

This lady in a supermarket is using a bar code reader.
Find the bar code on one of your goods.
Find out how it helps people.

In groups of 4, play in your shop.
Invent a system for your stock to help you work out what you have.
You could use your computer.
Each of you could have different jobs.

Is yours a good system?
Is it a modern system or an old-fashioned system?